A Counselor's Prayer Book

Kathleen Fischer
and
Thomas Hart

Paulist Press
New York   Mahwah

Published by Paulist Press
997 Macarthur Boulevard
Mahwah, New Jersey 07430

Printed and bound in the
United States of America

Library of Congress Cataloging-in-Publication Data

Fischer, Kathleen R., 1940–
    A counselor's prayer book/Kathleen Fischer and
Thomas Hart.
        p.   cm.
    ISBN 0–8091–3453–5 (paper):
    1. Pastoral counseling—Prayer–books and
devotions—English.   2. Spiritual direction—Prayer-
books and devotions—English.   3. Catholic Church—
Prayer–books and devotions—English.   I. Hart,
Thomas N.   II. Title.
BX2170.P33F57   1994
242'.692—dc20   93–37483
                                                        CIP

TABLE OF CONTENTS

SECTION TWO: FOR THE COUNSELOR AND COUNSELEE

SECTION THREE: FOR THE COUNSELEE ALONE

SECTION FOUR: RITUALS OF HEALING

INTRODUCTION

A growing number of people who seek counseling today want their faith to be an integral part of the process. They are looking for wholeness, and find it hard to put their relationship with God on hold while they deal with other issues. Many counselors, too, want their work with people to more fully reflect an awareness that God is present with us all in the healing journey.

This desire for integration reflects an expanding cultural conversation between the psychological and the spiritual, an acknowledgement on the part of many professions that our spiritual beliefs are powerful factors in the movement toward wellness. This dovetails with our Christian conviction that God desires fullness of life for us and continually offers us the grace which makes this possible. In Jesus we have a model of human wholeness, and in his resurrection the assurance of its final fulfillment.

The prayers and rituals in this book offer a way of making the spiritual dimension of counseling explicit.

We begin with prayers intended to support the spiritual life of counselors themselves. Such prayer connects our work with our faith, keeping us attuned to God in our own journeys as well as in our counseling sessions. These prayers for the counselor are followed by two collections of prayers: the first to be said with those who come for counseling, the second by counselees on their own. The final section contains the basic structure of a number of rituals we have found helpful in our own work, and which we hope will provide you with ideas for planning similar rituals for the persons you see.

A few practical suggestions: The prayers for counselor and counselee, and those for the counselee alone, are mutually adaptable to either situation. When praying for someone in a session, you might wish to lay hands on the person, or to hold their hands as you pray. Silences can also be very prayerful, and either of you may feel moved to pray in your own words. The rituals are relatively simple symbolic actions designed to accomplish some therapeutic task in a prayerful context. They usually come at the end of therapy on an issue, and are meant to bring closure. They are generally designed to be done in the counselor's office. But some counselees may choose to do them elsewhere, alone or with supportive friends.

Since there is great diversity among people who come for counseling, we have varied the structure, context, and ways of addressing God in all these prayers. Any item proposed can be altered to better fit a particular situation. Our hope is that they will open you and your counselees to the place of prayer in your journey together, and suggest ways in which you yourselves might creatively expand and deepen it.

SECTION ONE:

FOR THE COUNSELOR
ALONE

Sent to Minister

Jesus our healer, you send us into the world

>   *to make God's love visible,*
>   *to continue your ministry of healing,*
>   *to discover the joy and the cost of discipleship.*

I will go—carrying with me

>   *the promise of your befriending presence,*
>   *your empowering Spirit,*
>   *the hope of resurrection,*
>   *the peace which passes understanding.*

For Guidance

Dear God, often I do not know
    when to speak
    how to be silent
    where to focus
    what to say.

Give me wisdom
    to listen with a discerning heart,
    so that I can find
    a path of healing
    in a confusion of words.

Morning Meditation

As I begin my day of counseling,
I hold up to you, O God, each person I will see.
I contemplate them, and I pray for them.

As I reflect prayerfully on each one:

> *I ask you to bless them, to heal them,*
> *to free them from what binds them,*
> *to sustain them on the path of growth.*

(Pause)

What do I appreciate about this person
> *(couple, family)?*
> *Have I ever told them?*

(Pause)

What do I find difficult about this person?
> *What does this say about me?*
> *What does this say about them?*
> *Is there some way I can use this emotional*
> *information to help them?*

(Pause)

What does this person need now, as I see it?
> *How can I foster this today?*

(Pause)

Thank you, God, for my work.
Thank you for these particular people.
Be with me as I try to help them today,
that your purpose might be fulfilled both in them
and in me.

Centering before a Session

Let me be at peace within myself, receptive, open.

(Silence)

Free me of the internal noise that scatters my attention.

(Silence)

Open all my senses to hear both words and silences.

(Silence)

Prepare me to know this person emotionally, to enter into his (her) experience.

(Silence)

Make me aware that you are the source of life within us all.

(Silence)

Fill me with your great compassion toward myself and all beings.

(Silence)

Create in me a welcoming love and a discerning wisdom.

(Silence)

Blessing on the Day's Work

O God, as I approach another day of counseling—

I give you thanks and ask your blessing.
  Thank you for the gift of my work,
  for the privilege of coming to know others so
    deeply,
  and of being with them at the heart of their lives.
  Thank you for work that teaches me so much,
  that challenges and stretches me relentlessly,
  that uses and develops the talents you have given
    me,
  and rewards me so richly besides.

Thank you for the people you have sent me,
  the large number I love easily,
  the small number who test my love.
  Thank you for those who have taught and
    mentored me,
  and those who support and assist me when I need
    it.

Lover and Healer, be with me today,
  that I might be lover and healer too.
  Fill me with your Spirit,
  so that in me people may know something of you.

Give me openness, understanding, compassion,
affection, wisdom, and hope.
Help me to embrace, reverence,
nurture, and challenge each person as Jesus did.
Make me a channel of your peace.

For Compassion

Divine Friend of all beings,
Source of compassion and care,
   may my heart be home to you,
   filled with your steadfast love.

May I feel your presence guiding me in fear and
      doubt.

May your strength and wisdom be mine when I need
      them.

And may I walk always in humility and hope.

Prayers of Affirmation

I join myself with your deepest healing rhythms in all the life of the universe, listening to and contributing to their role in your work of creation.

When all around me seems dark, I know that your Light continues to shine.

In the strength of your Spirit I release all self-doubt and anxiety, all my preoccupations and distractions.

I trust my intuition and inner wisdom, believing that your power and insight dwell within me.

I trust that beyond the pain there is healing; and beyond the brokenness, wholeness.

I am a unique and valuable person. I need only do the best my awareness permits.

You have told me to love others as I love myself. The better I care for myself, the more I will be able to care well for others.

You are a healing power larger than my resources. I believe you will work within and beyond my efforts.

In your love, I can be aware of my limitations and accept them peacefully. Even my limitations are somehow an asset.

I affirm the beauty and wonder of every helping relationship and the mystery of my role as helper.

I let go of negative images of myself and listen likewise for the true voice of others. I believe that I show forth your image as does each of my clients.

I acknowledge and am grateful for each of the good things happening in my work. I count on your continued blessings.

A Meditation on Jesus as Listener

A woman enters Simon's house carrying an alabaster
    jar of ointment.
Weeping, she comes up behind Jesus and anoints his
    feet.
Those who see it condemn her, but Jesus hears the
    heart of one who loves much.
She leaves with a peaceful heart (Luke 7:36–50).

He arrives by night, afraid to be seen.
Nicodemus has questions about signs and spirits,
    water and new life.
Jesus loves this earnest, searching man,
    receives his confusion, and suggests a whole new
    way of seeing things (John 3:1–21).

She meets him at the well,
    her life like the shards of a broken jug,
    a woman clinging to the past, searching for
    salvation.
Jesus hears how deep is her thirst, how parched her
    soul.
She learns to drink again of living water,
    and leaves restored to her people (John 4:1–30).

He is too short and climbs a tree to see.
His past not right either—that of a despised tax
    collector.

Jesus welcomes Zaccheus joyfully, just as he is.
A changed man, he pays back all his debts,
    and gives to the poor besides (Luke 19:1–10).

All who came to you, Jesus, felt heard,
    understood, accepted.
They left closer to wholeness and hope.
May those who open their hearts to me
    find a like welcome.
May I learn to listen and love as you did.

A Psalm of Praise

Creator God,

I praise you for the privilege of witnessing the
wonders of the human spirit, and for the gift of
sharing the hidden depths of the human heart.

Blessed are you for inviting me to be with others as
they find the courage to remember painful pasts
and mourn terrible losses.

Blessed are you for allowing me to be present with
persons as they accept difficult truths, and begin
again after setbacks and disappointments.

Blessed are you for permitting me to share in
moments of forgiveness, in reconciliation after
years of alienation.

Blessed are you for giving me the gift of witnessing
others' hope in the midst of darkness and their
faith in times of uncertainty.

Blessed are you for asking me to hold both laughter
and tears, and listen to the rich imagery of
dreams.

The human person is indeed a work of beauty and mystery,
   O God. Thank you for letting me know it so profoundly.

In Thanksgiving

I thank you, God,
  for glimpses of grace:

     A husband and wife beginning to talk,
       learning to love again;

     A homeless family finding housing,
       work, dignity;

     A woman daring to feel,
       touching her anger, sadness, and joy;

     An abuse survivor finding her power,
       experiencing hope;

     A troubled child naming the hurt,
       coming to like himself;

     A lonely man moving through despair,
       seeing reasons to live.

       (Pause to recall other moments
        for which I am grateful).

I witness these moments
  with gratitude.

For Help with a Difficult Person

God of my life, I'm having trouble with someone I
minister to.
He (she) puzzles and exasperates me.
I've rarely felt so challenged.

I'm put off. I'm insecure. I don't know what to do.
Do I dislike him because I see in him what I find hard
to accept in myself?
Is it that he seems to ask of me something I do not have,
or do not wish to give?

I know you sometimes send people to teach me
something, to help me grow.
I do want to be a better person.
But what is the lesson here?
That I can be intimidated, manipulated, seduced?
That I cannot help everyone, even though I'd like to?

Thank you, God, for a job that challenges me so.
In my better moments I can see the value even of this.
Above all I want to be honest,
with myself and others;

and always genuinely loving,
even when I do not like someone.

Help me find my way in this relationship,
so that something good can come from it for both
of us.

Am I Helping Anyone?

God of barren places,
    today I come before you feeling helpless and
        discouraged.
When I listen to the depths of suffering in the human
        heart,
    and the ways people hurt one another,
    I find myself overwhelmed and speechless.
You who are the hope of the world, give me hope.

Spirit of truth,
    show me what I need to let go of if I am to do
    your work with greater joy and energy.
Free me of my need for praise and appreciation.
Help me set aside my anxiety and my striving for
        perfection.
You who died and rose again, show me where I must
        die in order to bring forth life.

Jesus our teacher,
    am I really helping anyone?
Helping is mysterious, elusive.
Some days I think I catch its meaning; then it is gone.
Attune my heart to the incomprehensible rhythms of
        healing.
Accept my ministry and fill it with your power.

God of birth and life,
   you labor and suffer to bring forth the new
      creation.
Anoint me to be a bearer of your Good News,
   to share in your work of breaking the yokes that
      bind, and removing the walls that imprison.
Make your justice, your truth, and your love real in
      my own life and the lives of those with whom I
      work. Amen.

It's Impossible

Dear God,

 I've had it.
 There are too many problems,
  too many needy people,
  too much to carry,
  too much to do.

 I have come to the end of
  my energy,
  my abilities,
  my patience and courage,
  my hope.

Rescue me, O God.

Teach me to care for myself better and to trust you
  more,
  to laugh more often and heartily,
  to walk in the woods and by the water,
  and to learn the lessons of the lilies of the
   field and the birds of the air.

Burn-out

Spring of living water,

God of river and stream,

Come to the desert of my heart.

Bring me back to life.

When Heavily Burdened

As evening shadows approach,

I carry the sorrow of a world torn and rent—
   generations of pain passed from parent to child,
   emptiness searching for alcohol, random sex, fast
     food,
   hardness in hearts refusing to yield or be blessed,
   betrayals of trust by governments and churches,
   global hunger, poverty, and war,
   disease and death striking without warning,
     disregarding goodness and virtue,
   violence and evil larger than hope and
     imagination.

Life-giving Spirit, brooding over creation,
   Spirit of comfort and truth,
   embrace this bent and broken world,
   and lead us out of this valley of death.

Keeping Perspective

Keep me focused, God,
   on what I am doing and why I am doing it.

Keep me mindful
   that mine is only a bit part in the total scheme
      of things.
   You are God, the universe is yours,
   and the lives of all of us are in your hands.

I am not responsible for the people I counsel,
   but only responsible to them.
   I will give them my very best while I am with them,
   but then I will hand them over to you.
   For grace is everywhere, and helpers are many.
   They got along without me before we met,
   and they will get on fine when we are apart.

Keep me mindful
   that I need not have the answers for them, God.
   The answers are inside them, and I merely assist their
      birth.
   In the end you, O God, are the answer.

Let me never forget
   that I am not in this to make money,
   or to establish a name for myself on earth.

Nor can my goal be to please everyone.
My commitment is to serve these people as best
    I can,
and to be faithful to the truth.
I will listen to them with care,
and give them my honest responses.

Let me not be grandiose or over-responsible.
    That is when my ministry becomes too heavy
        for me,
    and I get in the way besides.
    Just make me a person who loves much,
    speaks a helpful word, and is happy to walk
        along.
    Keep me above all a God-seeker myself,
    more bent on living the gospel than on preaching it.

SECTION TWO:

FOR THE COUNSELOR
AND COUNSELEE

Opening Prayer

Gracious God,
  we believe you are with us here—
  inside us, between us, around us—
  and we ask your blessing as we begin our session
    today.

Lover of truth,
  help us to know ourselves,
  and give us the courage to tell each other the truth
    with love.
  Guide our exchange,
  so that we may fully grasp what you would have
    us see,
  and live it with all our energy.

Healer of the human spirit,
  renew our spirits today,
  with your own undying freshness.
  Tenderly touch those places where we hurt,
  and heal them with the balm of your love.
  Fill up our weakness with your strength,
  so that we may speak as you would have us speak,
  and accomplish the work you would have us do.

Jesus, Powerful Liberator,
free us from all that binds us,
that we may walk in the freedom of the children of
God.

A Centering Moment

As we begin,
  let us breathe deeply and center our minds and
    bodies.

(Silence)

Let us come into our bodies,
  becoming aware
  of the feelings, the tensions,
  the expectations we carry.

(Silence)

Let us come into this moment,
  ready to hear what is present in the depths of our
    hearts.

(Silence)

Let us attend to the silence,
  allowing it to deepen and unfold its mysteries.

(Silence)

Let us pause to center ourselves as we begin.

Beatitudes

Blessed are those who rise to greet each morning,
letting the living of one day be enough,
our path to you, O God.

Blessed are those who pardon themselves their
inattentions,
mistakes, and failings, opening to your divine
forgiveness.

Blessed are those who have eyes to see the simple
beauty of a daisy, the splendor of the setting
sun, the majesty of a mountain, and praise you
in these marvelous manifestations.

Blessed are those with ears to hear the gentle sound
of falling rain, the inner movements of their own
hearts,
the laughter of children at play, your voice within
all voices.

Blessed are those whose hearts welcome the love and
affection of others, feeling no need to earn it,
remembering that in the love of others we know the
power of your love for us.

Blessed are all who trust and believe that this human journey is a sacred journey, and that you, O God, are repeatedly encountering us on our way.

God's Hidden Presence

Hidden God,
*   you who work in the tragedies of our existence,*
*   bringing joy out of sorrow,*
*   hope out of despair,*
*   courage out of fear,*
*   growth out of difficulties,*
*   life out of death,*
*   we give thanks for your quiet power in the*
*   development of our lives.*

May we recognize you as the God of darkness as well
*   as light,*
*   the God in the gentle breeze as well as the*
*   whirlwind,*
*   the God whose presence comes in the pillar of*
*   cloud as well as in the pillar of fire,*
*   the God revealed in the life and death of your Son,*
*   Jesus.*

In you we trust that there can be healing after pain,
*   the gift of resurrection.*

Praise for the Blessings of Each Day

Blessed are you, God of Gifts, for the light of the
        rising sun that welcomes us,
    families and friends who cherish us,
    food and shelter that nourish and sustain us.

Blessed are you, Divine Artist, for the fresh green of
        trees and subtle shapes of clouds;
    countless colors of flowers, birds, and butterflies;
    brightness of moon and stars in night skies.

Blessed are you, God of Surprises, for delight in the
        faces of playing children,
    the release of humor and laughter,
    celebrations and parties, circuses and zoos.

Blessed are you, Designer of Dreams, for people of
        courage whose actions inspire us,
    moments of joy that refresh our hearts,
    the dying and rising of your Son, Jesus,
        who grounds us in hope.

We thank you, God for your presence in the ordinary
        events of our lives. May we learn to rejoice in
        the gifts of every day.

When the Counseling Seems Stuck

Loving God, we're stuck.
What should we do?
We turn to you, trusting in your care for us.
Help us to see what we're not seeing.
Show us the way through.

You have brought us so far.
You have always been with us.
We know you want what is good for us,
whatever makes us freer, happier, more whole.

Light of the World,
Light of our Lives,
Dispel the darkness in which we stumble.
Free us from what trammels us.
Send us on our way again.

Give us the insight or imagination we need.
the courage we lack,
the words we grope for.
Surprise and delight us with that freshness you bring
forth forever.
We place our trust in you.

When Someone Is Anxious

Gracious God, we believe you are with us here,
and mindfulness of you brings a feeling of comfort.
You are the One who holds the cosmos together,
containing all its chaos and confusion.

Look graciously, O God, on your daughter (son)
————————— ,
who suffers from anxiety.
She frets and worries, losing her calm.
Help her to let go and relax.

Invite her to turn over to you all that concerns her so,
and trust you to take care of it.
Heal her of trying so hard—
trying to take care of everyone, and solve everything.

Tenderly touch her heart, Gentle God,
giving her the sense of safety she needs.
Teach her that you are Lord of the future
and hold all things in your hands.

Assure ————————— that you enfold her life too,
and will always give her what she needs.
Tell her she need not worry, nor try to control,
but can turn all her cares over to you.

Incomprehensible God, your ways are beyond our
fathoming.
But in your servant Jesus you taught us
to place our trust in you,
and be as little children.

As Jesus slept in the boat in the midst of the storm,
may _____ lay her head on your shoulder,
and let soothing rest refresh her.
Caretaker of the Cosmos, give her heart tranquility.

Litany for an Abused Woman

Leader: *"For God's temple is holy, and that temple you are"* (1 Corinthians 3:17).

O God who weeps with us in our pain, look with love on this woman in agony from the violence inflicted on her body and spirit, and support her as she opens to seemingly endless sorrow.

Response: We remember the pain and look toward healing.

Leader: You who are our shelter in the storm, be a harbor of safety to her, as she learns again to trust her own goodness and truth, and to believe in the love of faithful friends.

Response: We cry out against betrayal and long for true community.

Leader: Righteous God, receive her anger, offshoot of a growing awareness of her sacredness and of the evil of what was done to her. Let it be empowering to her.

Response: We will name the sin of violence and commit ourselves to work for justice.

Leader: *You who are the nurturer of life, help her to appreciate all the ways in which she learned to survive, and show her how these strengths can lead her to new life.*

Response: *We feel the call to make life safe for all.*

Leader: *Spirit of integrity, heal the shame and blame that bind her heart and body. Let the wounds of the past be transformed into witnesses of the resurrection's power.*

Response: *We will stand with all who struggle to free themselves from the past and to believe that the future is yours.*

In Time of Sickness

Jesus, Lover and Healer of humanity,
　　here is ＿＿＿＿＿＿＿ , whom you love.
　　She (he) is sick.
　　Lay your gentle, powerful hands upon her,
　　and make her well.

Revive her spirit, Lord.
　　Restore her strength, so that she can serve you.
　　Give her back to her family, friends, and all she
　　　　enriches,
　　who miss her in the vital roles she plays.
You have told us to ask for what we want,
　　and you would do it.
　　And so we come in faith, and boldly make our
　　　　plea.

But if it be your will that she drink this cup,
　　your will be done.
　　Then may she join her sufferings with yours,
　　for the redemption of the world.

Jesus, Resurrection and Life,
　　raise her up, we pray.

For a Couple in Difficulty

God of Love,
look graciously upon _____ *and* _____
here,
whom you have given one another in marriage.

You have made marriage holy,
consecrating this highest form of human friendship.
It is your will that in a couple's committed love,
the quality of your own love might be manifest to all—
accepting, patient, kind, forgiving,
challenging and nurturing,
faithful even to death, though the beloved is a
sinner.

_____ *and* _____ *have reached*
for that ideal of love,
and often realized it,
blessing one another and all who know them.
Thank you for all that you and they together have
realized,
and for all the happiness they have had together.

Now they stand at a painful place in their relationship.
Disappointments and hurts have made it hard for them
to see the good in one another,

and to remember all that has been.
They stand together in pain,
wondering if their love can weather this storm.

Faithful God,
when they committed themselves to one another,
you committed yourself also to them.
Guardian of the deep, invisible bond of married love,
be with them now.
Help them to find the spirit, and the words,
to work through their hurt and anger,
to come to forgive and cherish one another again.
May your love supply what is now deficient in theirs.
May your undying hope rekindle their hope,
and move them to risk again.

Gracious God,
always laboring to bring forth Christ in us,
ever blessing us even in our agonies,
deepen the faith of _____ and _____ in
this difficult hour.
May they experience new birth together,
and live to glorify your name.

When Struggling with an Addiction

O God, the goal of our longing,
  we are restless and searching,
  seeking a comfort and peace that elude us.
We reach out for many things,
  asking them to satisfy this hunger within and fill
    this emptiness we feel.
But they are poor solutions,
  leaving us with self-reproach and shame,
  deepening the pain they were meant to soothe.

Yet we cannot seem to control our urge to turn to
    them again, forgetting that we found them false.
And again we are disappointed and cast down.

We come home at last to you,
  beggared and ashamed.
Turn us not away.
Only your love can embrace and heal our
    powerlessness and despair.
Only you can fill our emptiness and satisfy our deep
    hunger.

You have told us to seek your face;
  hear us as we pray.

It is you for whom we pine; hide not your face from
    us.
  Quiet our hearts. Set us free.

For Someone Feeling Suicidal

God, loving Maker of us,
   here is _____ whom you love.
   Her (his) suffering is deep.
   She thinks of destroying herself,
   seeing no other solution to her problems.

Take her in your arms, gracious God.
   Let her feel your tender love,
   how precious she is to you.
   Show her what a vital role she has to play in the
      life of the world.

Faithful Friend, all seems darkness and pain now,
   and _____ cries to you.
   Hear her prayer, and give her the strength she
      needs to get through this difficult time.
   Take her hand and walk with her,
   through this valley of darkness,
   into meadows of refreshment.

Creator of the universe,
   you have made all things good,
   and you love all the works of your hands.
   Renew _____ 's sense of the goodness of
      life,
   so great and precious a gift.

Let her walk again with joy in the beauty of your
    creation,
giving thanks for the wonder of life.
We believe in you,
just as you believe in us.

Visualization for Healing of Memories

Have individuals relax by taking up a comfortable position and focusing on their breathing for a minute or two.

When they have indicated they are relaxed, ask them to return to the scene of a painful memory. Suggest that they actually enter again into the details of the scene, getting back in contact with the sights, sounds, and smells of the place, and allowing the feelings to come back.

When they have indicated that they are reexperiencing the painful event, ask them to invite Jesus to join them there and help them. Have them take a moment to wait for him and allow him really to materialize with them in the scene. Then instruct them to listen to what he says and watch what he does.

Allow several minutes for this, asking individuals from time to time what is happening now. Only minimal guidance is required. If they are experiencing something good (healing), invite them to stay with that and really take it in. Support them by praying for them silently.

If they get stuck, have them ask Jesus for help with it. If Jesus fades away, ask if they would like to invite him back. If Jesus does not come, ask them to wait. If Jesus is not an apt God-symbol for them, let them substitute another good and wise person who loves them and has their best interest at heart.

When they feel finished, have them come back to the present and open their eyes.

Spend a few minutes processing the experience together.

Suggest that they deepen the grace given by coming back to it in their prayer in the following days.

For Someone with Low Self-esteem

Gracious God, in whom we live and move and have
our being,
here is _____ , whom you love.
She (he) does not love herself very much,
because of messages she received early in life.
She cannot see her goodness,
and does not feel her power.

Open her eyes,
so that she can see herself as you see her.
Let her feel your love,
so that she can begin to love herself.

Gentle God, you cherish all that you have made,
and take delight in the works of your hands.
Let _____ know the joy you take in her.
Show her her beauty,
and the many talents you have given her,
because you prize her and desire her happiness.

You often express your love through other people,
and show us through them our true possibilities.
Open _____ 's mind and heart so that she
can receive the affection and affirmation others would
like to give her,
and are already giving.

It is so hard for us, God, to believe in our own goodness.
We need your help.
Open _____ to that breakthrough she needs.
In you we place our hope.

A Psalm of Letting Go

Leader: We bring to you, O God, the burden of all
that we have thought we must be and do,
all the expectations we have carried for so
long.

Response: Source of all blessings, we long to live in
peace, freed by your living word.

Leader: We entrust to your love all the people we
have felt responsible for, all those we have
tried to help, to cure, to save, to change.

Response: Source of all blessings, we long to live in
peace, freed by your living word.

Leader: We give you the burden of guilt that has
weighed down our hearts, asking you to
melt it away in the warmth of your forgiving love.

Response: Source of all blessings, we long to live in
peace, freed by your living word.

Leader: We place in your care all the anxieties we
carry about the future, all the fears we feel
when we ponder our own lives and the lives
of those we love.

Response: Source of all blessings, we long to live in
peace, freed by your living word.

Leader: *We relinquish our efforts to please people, our preoccupation with what others might think of us, and our desire to have their approval and praise.*

Response: *Source of all blessings, we long to live in peace, freed by your living word.*

Loving God, through your Son you taught us that the seed that dies springs again to life, that if we want to save our lives we must let them go. Help us to choose life by surrendering those things that block the flow of our joy. We come before you in need and in trust. Hear us, we pray. Amen.

Facing an Important Decision

Open us, O God, to your presence here,
and give us your Holy Spirit.
We ask special assistance for _____ ,
who struggles with a difficult decision.
It is a decision with major implications for him(her)self
and others,
and he wants very much to choose well.

He seeks to do your will, O God, and looks to you for
light.
Help him to know what will be genuinely best,
both for himself and for all who will be affected.

We ask, Divine Counselor,
that you orient our hearts and minds to the living out
of your values,
and the accomplishment of your purposes.
Then guide our deliberations as we weigh possibilities.

It is hard to live with uncertainty,
and we long sometimes for a sign from heaven.
Help _____ to trust in the powers you have
given him for discerning what is good—
his mind, the signs of the times, and the help of others.
Guide him as he looks at all his options for furthering
your work in the world.

Lead him toward the one best suited to himself.

We believe, O God,
that usually the answers are found deep within us,
where our true selfhood is and you also dwell.
Answer _____ 's search finally with peace,
the sign that he is at one with himself and with you.
Help him to find more of himself and of you,
as he seeks to do what is best.

A Birthday Blessing

O God, your word is life.

> *Hear our prayer as we ask your blessing*
> *upon _____ , your friend who today*
> *celebrates her (his) birthday.*

We rejoice in the gift of years you have given her,
and give you thanks for enriching us
and our world with her life.

> *(A special candle is lighted)*

May this candle be a symbol of the fire of life we
wish for her now and every day.

Awaken the child within her,
and fill her years with wonder and joy.

Open her eyes to her uniqueness among all beings,
and show her your paths of wisdom.

Fill her with a passion for your justice,
and sustain her in acting on behalf of our world.

Be with her in times of sorrow,
and bear her up on eagle's wings.

God of the dance and festival,
join her in making this day a true celebration of
the gift of life.

Seeking Sexual Integration

O God, you made us sexual beings,
planting in us a deep physical and emotional longing,
that we might reach out and find our completion in
relationship, and share the gift of life.
Male and female you created us, and saw that it was
good.
We bless you for the wondrous, powerful mystery of
our lives.

Lover of all human beings, look graciously on _____
who struggles now with this deep need and restless
energy.
Help him (her) to accept, bless, and be comfortable
with this promising, challenging, beautiful part of
himself.

Help him to integrate his sexuality into his loving.
Teach him to appreciate and enjoy all the beautiful
persons you have created without ever hurting or
exploiting anyone.
Let him be free and affectionate yet always responsible
and care-ful.

Assure him he is not alone in his struggle,
that each of us must engage it,
but that the battle is worth fighting and winning.

Right now _____ *has trouble seeing his own goodness,*
and the wonderful possibilities for love and fulfillment that lie within him.
But you see them, God of our sexuality.
Bless, support, and guide him into the fullness of his sexual life.

Blessing for a Person with AIDS

Compassionate God,

look with love on _____ , whom we love and cherish. Our hearts are filled with sorrow because he (she) is living with AIDS. We grieve with him all the losses this already has brought, and are concerned about those that lie ahead. Therefore, we ask your blessing on him today.

Give _____ an ever stronger sense of your care for him, that it might sustain and comfort him always. Help him to know that you love him with an everlasting love that is faithful and tender.

Still the terror of his heart when fear arises and begins to take hold within. Let him hear the words of reassurance that you have spoken to your friends throughout time: Fear not, I will be with you.

Open his spirit to the beauty and the gifts of each day. Help him to live every moment, fully taking in all that it has to offer which is life-giving, nourishing, inspiring.

Free him from any burdens of guilt and anxiety. Speak your words of forgiveness and lift the weight of all that clouds his sense that you are there for him.

Heal him in all the ways that are in keeping with your purpose. We wish long life for him, and freedom from pain and suffering. May he experience the healing embrace of your Son, who restored people to themselves.

We ask your blessing, too, on all of us who love him. May we know how to support him well and be the sacrament of your care for him. Enliven us when we lose hope, and strengthen us when we are weary. Touch the hearts of those he loves who have not been with him. Bring them to his side.

We thank you for all the ways in which you have shown us your care, and for the blessings we have experienced through _____ , as he has allowed us to make this journey with him. We are grateful for all that he gives us. We pray this in your Son, who has told us that he is the resurrection and the life, and in your Spirit who creates and heals. Amen.

Struggling to Forgive Self

Gracious God, we know that you are with us,
and that you look upon us always with love.
Here is _____ , your son (daughter),
who struggles to forgive himself.

Toward others, he shows compassion.
Toward himself, he finds that so difficult.
Yet he too is made of clay, this child of Adam and Eve.
Help him to accept himself within the human condition.

Your son Jesus taught us to forgive.
Help _____ to forgive himself.
Jesus commanded us to love our neighbor as we love
ourself.
Help _____ to love himself as he loves his
neighbor.

He is good, this man you have sent to me,
and let me know in his deepest selfhood.
I see his goodness, and you see it.
Let him see it too, and rejoice in it,
and be kind to himself.

Jesus, he has heard you say,
"Be perfect as your heavenly Father is perfect,"
and taken these words very much to heart.

Help him to hear you say,
"Be compassionate as your heavenly Father is com-
passionate,"
to balance his understanding, especially in his own
regard.

Each of us is broken, God.
All of us are sinners.
Yet it is you who have made us,
and said that we are good.
Help _____ to embrace himself whole,
as you embrace every part of him,
and to live his life with more acceptance, peace,
and joy.

Blessing for a Troubled Family

Gracious Creator,

We ask you to look with love on this family.
They come to you bowed down by hurt and
    misunderstandings,
  in search of truth and healing.
They are troubled by the anger, pain, and
    discouragement they find in their hearts.
Embrace them and heal them.

God of our struggle,

You have given us birth and made us in your image.
Breathe your Spirit into each member of this family.
Do not allow fear, ignorance, or pride to limit the
    action of your divine creativity in them.
Show them your mercy and peace.

Christ our companion,

We give thanks for all the goodness in this family.
In this time of difficulty, do not let them lose sight of
    their beauty and gifts.
Help them to remember the good times and recognize
    the positive qualities each one has.
Restore them to wholeness.

Creator of new futures,

This family finds it hard to hope again.
Stay close to them and provide them with direction.
Show them the small steps that will bring change.
Encourage and support them when they fail.
Sustain them on the path of love.

Giver of life,

We bless each member of this family in your name.
You have invited all who are burdened to come
to you.
Receive them as they are, and show them what
they can be.
Remove their hearts of stone and give them
new hearts.
May their lives be renewed by the power of
your grace.

Awareness of Aging

Leader: O God, we come to you today to reflect on how you are present in all the cycles of our lives. We pray that we may be open to the graces of each of life's seasons.

Response: Teach us to number our days, O God, that we may gain wisdom of heart (Psalm 90:12).

Leader: We remember Sarah and Abraham who in their old age believed in your promise that emptiness would become fullness, who trusted that your faithfulness would make their future fruitful.

Response: Teach us to number our days, O God, that we may gain wisdom of heart.

Leader: We remember all those older persons in our midst who show us that at any age we can be instruments of renewal and reconciliation, bringing new life and hope to the entire human family.

Response: Teach us to number our days, O God, that we may gain wisdom of heart.

Leader: We remember Ruth and Naomi, Mary and Elizabeth, whose friendships reveal the *spiritual richness found in relationships that span the generations.*

Response: *Teach us to number our days, O God, that we may gain wisdom of heart.*

Leader: *We remember the wise man Simeon and the prophetess Anna who knew how to wait at every moment for the coming of God, and who heard the hidden presence of God in their time.*

Response: *Teach us to number our days, O God, that we may gain wisdom of heart.*

Leader: *We ask you to pour out your Spirit on us and on our world so that we may experience the promise of Pentecost, that our young men and women will see visions and our young men and women will dream dreams.*

Response: *Teach us to number our days, O God, that we may gain wisdom of heart.*

Closing:

We will sing the wonders of your love forever, O God;
*   we will proclaim your faithfulness to all generations.*
We will declare that your love is steadfast, your faithfulness fixed as the heavens.

Happy the people who have learned to acclaim you,
who walk in the light of your presence!
(Psalm 89:1–4,15)

On Receiving Bad News

O God,

We are stunned and shaken by this news.
It changes everything.
We struggle to take it in, to believe it is really true.
Fear and sorrow well up in our hearts.
Feelings chase one another inside us,
    mixing and churning.
Tightness and foreboding take hold of our bodies.
All the ordinary things we were thinking and doing
        are swept suddenly away,
    as with a high tide rising, a fierce wind blowing.

Stay with us. We are afraid and at a loss.
Like your people wandering in the desert,
    we know not which way to go.
Like your disciples huddled behind closed doors,
        shattered by news of your Son's death, we feel
        our courage ebbing away.
Give us strength to endure what lies ahead.
Help us to know what to do, how to respond.
Support all those who are touched by this news.
        Sustain them in this time of darkness and
        sorrow.

Embrace us all, God of Love, as we take the measure
        of this happening and seek ways to respond to it.

On Receiving Good News

Leader: We come to you, good and gracious God, our hearts filled with gladness. Blessed are you for giving us new reasons to hope. Good news has come today, and we are overjoyed.

Response: We give thanks, Bestower of Gifts, for the wonders of your love.

Leader: Searcher of Hearts, you know what this news means to us, how our spirits leapt when we heard it, how it has brightened the horizon of our lives.

Response: We give thanks, Bestower of Gifts, for the wonders of your love.

Leader: New energy fills us and we feel the warmth of your love. We have prayed to be open to your larger purpose, and we want to use the joy of this day to work for the fullness of your peace and healing in our world.

Response: We give thanks, Bestower of Gifts, for the wonders of your love.

Leader: Bless all who have loved and supported us as we waited for this news. May they share *in the joy of this day and may their own lives be richly blessed.*

Response: *We give thanks, Bestower of Gifts, for the wonders of your love.*

Leader: *Bless those who still long for a word of hope, who walk in faith and struggle with their burdens. May they soon share our happiness.*

Response: *We give thanks, Bestower of Gifts, for the wonders of your love.*

Leader: *Loving Creator, we know this good news is but one gift among the countless blessings you offer us. We thank you today for all that we take for granted and fail to notice: for the beauty of the earth and our daily bread, for health and work, for family and friends, and all good things.*

Response: *We give thanks, Bestower of Gifts, for the wonders of your love.*

Embracing the Darkness in Ourselves

God of darkness as well as light, help us to embrace all that we are. We want to dispel the darkness, the shadows we find within ourselves. Help us rather to bring these poles of light and darkness into unity and learn to be whole, perfectly ourselves, made in your image.

You who moved over the primeval waters, bringing light and darkness into the unity of a single day, still our temptation to judge the dark parts of ourselves harshly. Lead us to the awareness that our strengths and weaknesses cleave to one another as two aspects of the same energy, that our virtues and vices are intertwined.

You who make things lovable by loving them, teach us to listen to the dark energies in our emotions and relationships, to admit and feel our anger, resentment, melancholy, envy, and hate. May our ability to feel and accept all that we are enable us to act in less hurtful ways towards ourselves and others. Lead us in ways that are life-giving for ourselves and others. Keep us from paths of destruction and let the darkness fuel the goodness within us.

You who empower roots to grow in the cold darkness of earth, remind us that darkness is your dwelling place too. You met Moses in a thick cloud covering Mount Sinai. Clouds and darkness are your cloak, the psalmist says. In prayer we often meet you in the cloud of unknowing, a darkness akin to your mystery. Make us more comfortable with the darkness of waiting and hoping, not knowing what may come.

We praise you, God of darkness as well as light. Enfold and shelter us on our journey.

When a Session Ends Unfinished

O God,
  this was not one of our better sessions,
  and we come to the end of our time today unsettled
    and unsatisfied.
  It feels unfinished,
  and we don't know how to make it come right.

You, O God,
  seem more comfortable with quandary and tension
    than we are.
  Often in the past,
  you have blessed our perplexity and struggle with
    unexpected fruitfulness.

We call on you as we part today,
  to sustain us in the unease we feel,
  and make it somehow productive.
  Help us to be patient as this gradually sifts out,
  until we discern in it the truth you would have us
    see.

God of light, God of comfort,
  soothe our troubled spirits,
  deepen our trust,
  and gradually guide our steps toward
    understanding.

When a Session Ends Well

We give you thanks, O God,
for the way you have supported and helped us today.

We have felt your love,
working within the love we have for each other.

You have given us the courage to explore,
and we see more of the truth now.

Grace us as we part,
with the gift of your own Spirit,
that we may be further enlightened,
and strengthened,
to live the lives you want us to live.

May we always know your gracious love,
helping us to accept and love ourselves.

May we feel your healing power at work in us,
binding up our wounds, making us whole.

With the help of your light,
may we find more and more of our true selves.

Make us great lovers, O God,
as you are a great lover.

Make us creators and lifegivers, O God,
as you are so wonderfully for us all.

A Closing Blessing

May the peace of God
    dwell in your heart.

May the light of God
    shine in your darkness.

May the comfort of God
    soothe your inner being.

And may God be a strong rock
    on whom you can rely.

Section Three:

For The Counselee Alone

For Personal Integration

Perhaps I am not so much a person,
  as the raw materials for a person,
  and my life is the time of creation.

Perhaps every part of me has a value,
  even the parts I despise;
  and each has a crucial role to play in the story of
    my existence.

Creator of the Universe,
  Font of things strange and wonderful,
  Praise to you for the mystery of my being.

Help me put myself together.

Out of all the notes that play in me,
  even those that sound harsh now,
  help me to make a symphony both of us
    can enjoy.

A Lament in Time of Grief

Who will hear the cry of my heart?
I long for relief, but there is none.

Gathering clouds conceal the sun.
My world turns cold and grey.

People about me go on buying and selling.
Inside I call out: How can life go on as before?

I dwell in emptiness and dread.
Each day I wake with a heavy heart.

A moment of peace—then waves of anguish.
Sadness sweeps over me unannounced.

I am like a log buffeted by an angry sea.
Even you, my God, seem distant and unconcerned.

I cling to you,
though I do not always feel your presence.
Carry me through this time of grief.

You, O God, who weep with us in our pain,
You who know the sorrow I cannot find words
to express,
Stay with me as I move through this passage.
Be my Ark of safety on these stormy seas.

When Unemployed

O God who rejoices in both our work and our play,
  I come before you
    unemployed,
    afraid,
    shaken in my trust.

When I lose courage and hope while searching for
        work,
  be my rock of safety.

When I find it hard to believe in my talents,
  revive in me an appreciation of the gifts you have
        given me.

When I begin to doubt my worth,
  help me to remember that I do not need to earn
        your love.

When my fears take hold and start to overwhelm me,
  let me find comfort in your care for me and those I
        love, and in their love for me.

Thank you for all those who continue to support and
        encourage me during this difficult time.
  May it somehow bring us closer to one another and
        to you.

Preparing for a Difficult Conversation

O God, you have shown us the power of your Word
 to heal and unite, to bring insight and
 reconciliation. Be with me now as I prepare for
 this talk with my (parent, child, spouse, friend,
 employer).

I am anxious as I think about this conversation,
 and fearful that I will not know what to say,
 or will say it poorly.
I feel afraid when I imagine the responses I may
 receive.
I draw back, ready to settle for distance,
 misunderstanding, things as they are.

You search the depths we cannot know.
 Let me listen beyond the words and in the silence.
 May I catch what others do not say, but only feel
  and think.
 Open my heart to the kind of receptivity that
  deepens communication.
 Strengthen me to bear the pain and disappointment
  I may experience.
 Teach me to trust that conflict can lead to growth
  and renewal.

Jesus, your word is truth and life.
Help me find the words I need to speak.
Give me courage to tell the truth with love.
Ground and center me so that my speech may create a bridge to greater understanding and acceptance.

Come now, Spirit of integrity, fill my heart with the energy of your love, and fire my words with the power of your truth. Touch and help all who will be a part of this conversation. Our hope is in you.

A Caregiver's Prayer

"In meadows of green grass you give me repose;
beside restful waters you lead me" (Psalm 23:2).

Jesus, you cared for all the sick
who came to you.
I want to care with loving compassion,
to attend to details with gentleness.
But I become weary and impatient,
angry and abrupt.
It is hard to watch the suffering of someone I love,
hard to find energy for all I must do.
I grow discouraged and resentful.
Let me learn from your life of compassion.

"May your kindness, O God, be upon us,
who have put our hope in you" (Psalm 33:22).

Spirit of healing and comfort,
Be with me in these difficult times.
Teach me to take time for myself,
to be gentle with my own limits,
to ask for help from others.
May your grace allow me
to forgive myself when I fail,
to let go of my expectations,
to grieve all my losses.

Send your healing power to me and the one for
whom I care. We trust in your love.

"Send out your light and your truth,
let these be my guide" (Psalm 43:3).

A Woman's Creed

I believe that I am created in the divine image,
    that my body and spirit are holy.
    The God who dwells in all of creation lives in the
    inmost depths of my being.

I believe that I am loved by God just as I am,
    without conditions or demands that I be more.
    I am enough. This love sustains me when I am in
    doubt and upholds me when I fail.

I believe that God desires my freedom and wholeness,
    the full expression of my talents. I need not live
    by the values of others, nor silence my self to
    please them. I can let my own voice ring out, my
    own song be sung. I can trust what I feel and
    know, living out of my own deepest truth.

I believe in the power of women to heal and love, to
    seek truth and justice. This faith is strengthened
    when I remember the women throughout time
    who have used their power and gifts to change
    the world: Sarah, who answered God's call;
    Esther and Deborah, who saved a nation; Mary
    Magdalene and the other women, who
    announced the resurrection in the face of
    skepticism.

I believe that my gifts and strengths are for cherishing myself, others, and the world. The more I care for myself, the better I will be able to care for all living beings.

Being Gay

O God, I am gay (lesbian).
   I have fought against it for a long time,
   denied it, tried to change it.
   I see now it is a fact I must accept.

It is not easy, God.
   Some people in my church condemn me;
      they say you condemn me.
   Society is filled with hatred and violence
      against me.
   Those who understand and accept people
      like me are few.

I have heard it said
   that I should rejoice in being gay;
   that gay is good and beautiful,
   that it is part of your creation.

That is not so easy though.
   I am different from the majority,
   and constantly made to feel it.
   Either I come out, and face all possible
      consequences,
   or live in hiding, protecting my secret,
   and pretending I am something I am not.

I want to believe that you love me, God,
that you have made me as I am,
and that you support me in the difficult life
I face.
That does not make it easy,
but it makes it bearable, meaningful.

God of human diversity, bless me,
and help me to bless myself.
Help me to live a good life.
Guide my sexual decisions.
And let me contribute to the arduous task of
bringing all people to celebrate
the richness of human diversity.

When Angry with God

O God with whom I wrestle,
  I struggle to let myself express the anger I feel
    toward you.

My head tells me that you are large enough to receive
      all that I am,
  but it is hard to come before you like a churning
    cauldron, full of ugly energies.

Though I try to quiet them, my feelings heat up and
      boil over. I want to make a fist and shake it,
        crying out against the world you have created,
  and shouting, "Where are you now, when we need
    you?"

I sought your presence, but you were like a total
      stranger—remote and unavailable. I implored
      your help,
  but nothing changed. Though I have tried to follow
    your ways and remain faithful to your call, it
    has done me no good at all.

Like Jeremiah, I say that you duped me and I let
      myself be duped.
Like Martha, who sent for Jesus when her brother lay
      dying, I cry out in protest.

*Help me to believe that this wrestling keeps me in
    honest, lively relationship with you,
  that I would not be angry with you if you did not
    matter so much to me.*

*Help me to trust that as this cauldron of my rage
    empties into the embrace of your love,
  I will continue to trust in you, my God.*

For a Stronger Sense of Self

O God, so often I feel powerless in the world,
as if I lack the means to claim my place and do my task.
Everyone else seems stronger, surer,
and I shrink back in fear.

I withhold what I think,
fearing people will laugh, or tell me I'm wrong.
I don't say what I want or need,
convinced I'll be ignored.

Where was I when courage was given out?
Why do I feel I am nothing,
that everybody has stature but me?

Heal me, God.
Help me find the parts of myself I've lost or never
acknowledged.
Surely I have worth, and right, and power,
and can take a stand and exert an influence.

Teach me, Jesus, the meaning of your saying that the
meek shall inherit the earth.
Show me the sense of Paul's proclamation that God has
chosen the foolish ones of this world to confound
the wise,
and the weak ones of this world to confound the strong.

In you I am grounded, O God.
Let your life and strength course through me.
Reveal to me what I am,
and help me to play my part.

A Meditation in Time of Transition

THERE IS A SEASON FOR EVERYTHING,
A TIME FOR EVERY OCCUPATION
UNDER HEAVEN
(Ecclesiastes 3:1–5).

A TIME FOR GIVING BIRTH, A TIME FOR DYING. . . .

*O God who brought us to birth, I have
let go of the old and cannot see the
new. Sustain me in this time of darkness
and waiting. I do not know what is to come.*

A TIME FOR PLANTING, A TIME FOR UPROOTING. . . .

*O God the font of insight, be with me as
I search out the truth of this passage. Give
me clarity to know what is best, and courage
to choose it.*

A TIME FOR TEARS, A TIME FOR LAUGHTER. . . .

*God of all trust, you have promised that
sadness will be turned to joy, despair to
hope, death to life. In this wintry season,
keep me attentive and alert to the signs of
spring.*

A TIME FOR THROWING STONES AWAY,
A TIME FOR GATHERING THEM UP. . . .

God of wisdom, our time is in your hands.
May the future bring us, with all of your
creation, closer to your vision of beauty
and peace. I trust in your word.

Dealing with a Difficult Child

God, Parent of us all,
we feel at such a loss with our child.
We do not know how to deal with him (her).
Nothing we try seems to work.

He is your gift to us, and has brought us much joy.
We thank you for him.
You made him, and saw that he was good.
Indeed he is good, and we love him.

But we worry about him, God.
We do not like the behavior we see,
or the direction he is taking.
How do we change it?
He fights us, hurts us deeply,
and leaves us feeling like total failures.

Are we on the wrong track?
Are we trying to make him into something he is not?
Do we fail to see what is there, or hear what he is trying
to say to us?
Are we impatient? Or too demanding?

We turn to you, God, with anguished hearts.
Bless and be with our son.
Give him what we cannot supply.

Touch his heart.
Show him the way.

We pray for ourselves.
Teach us patience, understanding, wisdom.
Help us to be faithful to him, and to each other.
Teach us to forgive injuries, and remain largehearted.

Lover of families, bless our family,
and hold us in your care.
Keep us mindful that there is a blessing for all of us in
this painful struggle.
Mold us and fashion us through it,
according to your purpose.
Weary and at a loss, we place our trust in you.

Wanting to Forgive

Merciful God, help me to forgive.
I've been carrying this anger a long time,
and it is eating me up.
I'm the person it's hurting, not the person who hurt me.

It was a terrible wrong and completely unfair.
It has cost me dearly.
But it is old, God, and I know it's time to let it go.
I need your help.

Jesus, you teach forgiveness,
and the example of your own life moves me.
You forgave those who crucified you,
as well as Peter, your friend.
Give me your incredible spirit.
Take this heart of stone, and give me a heart of flesh.

I know forgiving doesn't mean condoning,
or allowing people to treat me badly.
I know it doesn't mean pretending it never happened,
or that it didn't make much difference.
But it does mean letting it go,
letting it fade into the past,
not using it against the person anymore,
giving another chance.

I'm getting there, God, but it is still beyond me.
Take me the rest of the way.

God of mercy, you have forgiven me so many times.
Help me now to see the person who hurt me
as you see him (her);
to view him in his context,
so I can understand and be compassionate.
Father of Jesus, help me to forgive.

Lament over the World

My heart is heavy, God, as I think about the world.
    There is so much suffering.
    Hungry people. Refugees. Prisoners.
    Broken families. Lonely folks.
    Women oppressed. Children abused.
    A few have so much, while many lack the means
        of life.
    Governments spend for arms,
    and let their people languish.
    Always there is war,
    and the wealthy rape and plunder the earth.

Sometimes I feel angry at you, God, for letting this
        go on.
    Then I feel angry at myself and everybody else,
    for the same reason.
    Why do so few seem to care?
    Do you care? You must, for you are a lover.
    Surely you weep, as Jesus did, over this world.

Sometimes I think you have shared your heart
        with me,
    giving me part of your passion.
    But sometimes I think I'm trying to carry what is
        not mine, since I am not God.
    Perhaps you want me to be a little child,

to admit I don't understand, and never will,
to put my trust in you and be at peace.

Help me to do all I can, God,
to lessen injustice and alleviate suffering.
Make me part of the solution instead of part of the
problem.
May I follow Jesus' example, doing all I can,
trying to get others to join in,
and entrusting the rest to you.

Come to our assistance, God.
May your will be done on earth, as it is
in heaven.

In Sickness

This room has become my world,
and it seems very small.

I am prisoner of this body, and it no longer works.
 I live in pain's embrace, and need others to do for
  me what I long to do for myself.

God, I know you are with me,
 but I wish I could feel it more.

I know it is time for me to go within,
 that my world is there now, and you are
  there too.
 It is time to be with you,
 to reflect on my life,
 to pray for those I love, and for the whole world.

Illness has stripped me, God,
 and my life is very simple now.
 Don't let me sink into self pity,
 or be a burden to others.
 May I somehow be a grace to those who visit and
  minister to me.

Jesus, I join my sufferings with yours.
Turn them to some good for me and for others.
I will try to follow you now in bearing my cross,
with courage and with hope.

For Healing from Sexual Abuse

You know, God, that as a child I was sexually
  abused.

  I lost my childhood.
  I lost my good family.
  I lost my physical integrity.
  I lost my honesty.
  I lost my trust.

I have carried this trauma in my body and deep
    inside my spirit
alone for many years.
Now it is out,
and I am beginning to heal.
Thank you for my counselor and friend who has
    opened me, accepted me, supported me, given
    me hope.

  I am wounded, God, and I have begun to bleed.
  Immense sadness sweeps through me.
  I feel shame, though I know it was not
    my doing.
  I feel rage.
  It is hard for me to trust anyone with my
    fragile self.

Comfort me, Gracious God.
Hold me as I weep.
Raise me up, and restore my sense of wholeness.
Let your grace course through me,
and restore my sense of holiness.

I know you didn't want this, God,
for me or anyone else.
You stand with me in my grief,
and labor with me for my healing.

Open me to the people who really love me,
and make me feel safe again.
May I be a protector of the young,
and a compassionate healer of hearts.

Bringing Anger to God

O God, I feel angry all the time,
and I don't know why.
I take it out on friends and family,
hurting those I love.

What is really bothering me?
Am I hurt? Frustrated? Afraid?
Am I simply exhausted?
Or am I unhappy with the shape of my life?
I know this anger is information, and I want to listen.
But I'm having trouble getting to the bottom of it.

Help me, God, to get beneath the outer crust,
to find those deeper places in myself,
where I am sad, thwarted, or scared.
Help me to name whom I am angry at,
and what I am angry about.
Then show me what I must do to set my life aright.

Jesus, you felt anger, and you freely expressed it.
I love that in you. It helps me.
Often we have good cause for anger,
and need its energy to address what is wrong.

I ask your assistance, God.
Help me to discern truly—

to know when to protest, when to remove myself,
when to change my attitude and not let things bother
me so.
Teach me to judge what is mine and what is not.
Help me to come to more peace.

When a Spouse Dies

O God, she (he) is dead, she is gone,
the best friend I ever had,
My world is empty. Nothing matters.
I find no joy in anything, and wish I could die myself.

Everywhere I turn I see her,
and up come my tears again.
My nights are restless, long,
and all my days are grey.
The ache inside is huge, gaping,
the only thing I feel.

I was not a perfect husband, God. You know that.
How sorry it makes me now.
Why couldn't I see how good and precious she was?
I would have curbed the sharp word,
and let the little things go.
I would have told her and showed her more often how
much I loved her.

O God, I don't know what to do.
There seems nothing left for me.
I am a burden to myself, and no good to anyone.

Jesus, Healer of Souls, I need you as never before.
Reach down to me and pull me to my feet.
Call me from the tomb. Breathe on me that I may live.

When a Child Dies

Dear God, our child has died.
We are stunned, stricken, devastated.
She (he) was beautiful, special, full of life,
a gift we cherished even before she was born,
and from there the love just grew.

How could you allow this to happen?
Our finite minds are baffled,
and anger smolders with our sadness.
Other children seem to thrive.
This child, lovely with promise, is no more.

"The Lord gives, and the Lord takes away;
blessed be the name of the Lord."
Is that supposed to console us?
We can't believe it, God of our faith, we cannot be-
lieve it.

You, Wonderful Maker, fashioned this child with care
and gave her the breath of life.
Fullness of life is your wish for us all.
We believe you grieve with us, Mother/Father God,
Devoted Parent, Lover of humanity.
We believe your tears mix with ours, and you stand by
us in our grief.

This, like so many awful things that happen,
must have been beyond your control.
And now, with us, you work to bring some good
from it,
as you did with the tragic death of your faithful servant
Jesus.

We believe in eternal life, O God,
and trust that our child enjoys it now with you.
But our loss is keen, searing, unfathomable.
Hold us, O God. Hold us singly, and hold us together.
Help us recover from this terrible blow.
Give us the strength to go on.

Mend, O God, our broken hearts.
Into your hands we commend our spirits.

In Time of Loneliness

God, I'm lonely.
My heart aches.
It seems I've always been lonely,
and I see no remedy.

I wish you would be my friend, Great One.
I reach for you, but I do not feel you.
Are you with me?

Even sharing this ache with you somehow helps.
Maybe you are here; maybe you do care.
Your silence somehow comforts me.
Maybe if I weren't lonely, I wouldn't look for you
at all.

Is everyone lonely, God?
Are there people who need me perhaps,
as badly as I need companions myself?
How do we find one another, become friends?
Am I so alone because I don't reach out?
Do I present myself as unavailable, or pretend I'm
just fine?

It is hard for me, God, to believe anyone could love me.
What do I have to give?

I feel empty. I'm not very interesting.
And so I hide.

Help me to believe in myself, God.
Give me the courage to smile and say hello.
Send me someone who needs me,
or who could be my friend.

Lover of the human family,
help me to join the human family and feel that I belong.
Help me to set aside my fear,
and reach out for what I need.

Please be my friend yourself—Faithful One.
Above all others, for you my heart thirsts.

In Depression

O God, I feel so depressed.
  I don't want to get up in the morning.
  Nothing interests me,
  and sadness sits on me like a cloud.

I cannot think clearly when I am like this, God.
  Please give me the help of good friends.
  I need your aid too, my God
  I lift up my eyes to the mountains.

Surely you want me to be happy, Giver of life.
  You will help me get through this.
  Help me to stop thinking so negatively,
  and being so hard on myself.
  Open my eyes to all that is good in my life,
  to everything that is going well.

Give me some energy, Powerful One.
  I've got to get active again.
  I need to make some changes in my life—
  to eliminate what drags me down,
  to find those things that nourish my spirit.

Jesus, healer of hearts,
  lay your hands on me and cast out this disease.
  I'm weary of it, bone sick of it,
  yet I feel so helpless.

Let your healing power flow through me.
  Strengthen me, so I can pick up my mat
    and walk.
  Let me live to sing your praise.
  Jesus, Resurrection and Life, raise me up again.

Thanks and Praise for Life

Gracious Creator, thank you for the gift of life.
I say it not because my heart is full of joy today,
but because I want to be mindful of what I often forget—
that life is a precious gift,
and the ordinary is filled with the wonderful.

Thank you for the marvel of my body,
its basic health and strength, its freedom of movement,
its amazing senses, its many skills, its sexuality.

Thank you for the wonder of my mind,
for the gift of education, for the light of understanding,
for the infinite horizon of my awareness.

Thank you for this world, so full of beauty and precious things.
May my eyes and ears be open, and all my faculties alert,
that I may relish and give praise for such abundant goodness.

Thank you for all the people I live, work, and talk with.
Each is a mysterious world, as I am myself.
May I appreciate and reverence them,
enrich them somehow, and take in what they have for me.

Thank you for my faith, my relationship with you.
It supports and sustains me. It shows me the way.
It helps me accept myself, and this troubled world,
with equanimity.

Preserve in me, Great God, a keen sense of wonder.
Let me never lose my sense of play.
Keep my step light, my laugh ready, my affection
abundant.
Life is short, and it is happening now.
Help me get both my feet into the dance.

Section Four:

Rituals of Healing

Goodby to Someone Who Oppresses Your Spirit

This ritual enacts a psychological/emotional separation from a problem person—e.g., an abuser, critical parent, tragic relative—who remains a negative influence.

Opening Prayer

Gracious God, we open ourselves to your presence and your empowering Spirit. Help us as we begin this ritual of separation. Give us the healing we need, and set our spirits free. We ask it in Jesus' name. Amen.

Reading: Rm 8:28–39, Rm 14:7–11, Mt 8:16–22, or Mt 9:1–8

Play some meditative music as you reflect on the reading and the relationship. Briefly share your thoughts.

Farewell

Read a letter of farewell to some symbolic representation of the person. Then place the symbol of the person next to a symbol of God.

Prayer: God of compassion and mercy, into your hands I commend ＿＿＿＿＿＿ .

Ours was a difficult relationship, and I have tried to make it right without success. Now I entrust him (her) to you, his maker and judge, for I need to say goodby and get on with my own life. You know what he needs, and you know what I need. Be gracious to us both, faithful God. I ask it in Jesus' name. Amen.

Blessing

Counselor lays hands and blesses you:

God of resurrection and new life, give _____ your blessing. Deepen the healing that has begun here today. Your will is always life for us, and liberation. Having freed _____ from the burden that oppressed her, send her on her way with lightness of spirit and lasting peace. May she praise you for the rest of her days. Through Christ our Lord. Amen.

Strengthening Family Bonds

A Favorite Family Song

Opening Prayer

> Gracious Parent God, Father and Mother of families, we gather in your presence hoping to strengthen the bonds among us. Thank you for our family, for our history together, for each of our members. Bless us and guide us, so that our life together may be a visible enactment of your love. We ask this in Jesus' name. Amen.

Reading: Col 3:12–17, or I Cor 13:1–7, or Mk 10:13–16

Appreciation: Focusing on each person in turn (person in focus holds a lighted candle), everyone in the family circle says something they love and appreciate about him or her. It could be a personal quality, or something they do for the family, or something they achieved recently. These should be written in advance, and, after they are spoken, left with the person addressed.

Reconciliation: Any member of the family who feels a need to be reconciled with anyone else seeks reconciliation with that person.

> Then all join hands and pray: God of compassion and mercy, we love one another; but we fail and hurt each other sometimes too. By the example of your great mercy, help us to forgive, to accept each other, and to live in peace. We ask it in Jesus' name. Amen.

Creative Imagining: Each person expresses some wish they have for family life—e.g., that we play more together, or pitch in better on chores, or share feelings more openly. These ideas are all just listened to respectfully, without any reply. They can be explored more later.

Blessing: Each person in turn stands or kneels in the center of the family circle, and everyone else lays a hand on them and prays:

> _____ , may God bless you and keep you. May God protect you from harm

and be close to you. May God give you what your heart most deeply desires, and help you become the person God envisioned in creating you. Amen.

An embrace all around

Renewal of Marriage Covenant

Opening Prayer

God, our loving creator, your fidelity to us has brought us, by a route filled with unusual stories, to this new embracing of one another in love. We praise and thank you with all our hearts. We come today to renew and celebrate our covenant with one another and with you. Strengthen us and bless us as we continue our journey together. And help us to be a blessing to others.

Reading: Eph 3:14–21, or 1 Jn 4:7–12, or Col 3:12–17

Play some meditative song as you reflect on the reading and your relationship. Briefly share your thoughts.

New Covenant

Vows: (Join hands) _____ , I take you for my husband (wife). I promise to love you faithfully all the days of my life. I want my love to mirror Christ's love for you—true, patient, kind, self-sacrificing, in

good times and in bad, a creative and renewing force in your life. Together with you, I
want to grow in the life we share as follow-
ers of Jesus Christ. (Say in turn)

Rings: _____ , accept this ring as
a sign of our marriage. May it always remind
you of my love for you.

Candles: From an already lighted candle
symbolizing God's presence, partners light
their separate candles simultaneously. They
draw them to themselves a moment, then
merge them together into one. Holding
them separately again, they pray:

We give you thanks, gracious God, for
bringing us to this day. Thank you for our
love, which by your aid has survived so
many challenges and enjoys this rejuvena-
tion. Abide with us always, holding us together, keeping us growing, making our
home a place of peace and hospitality. We
ask it in Jesus' name. Amen.

Blessing: Counselor lays hands on the couple and prays:

> God, I thank you for letting me witness this event. To it I lend all my support. Bless ___ and _____ on this wonderful occasion. Sustain them on their continuing journey with your faithful love and assistance. Through Jesus Christ our Lord. Amen.

An embrace all around

Bringing Good Out of Evil

Reading: Ephesians 3:16–21

(Pause to light a candle)

Opening Litany

> *Leader:* We remember, God, that in the beginning of creation you brought life and light from darkness and chaos. We believe you continue to help us find meaning in adversity.

> *Response:* Blessed are those who see the light shining in the darkness.

> *Leader:* Through your Son, Jesus, you showed us that life comes out of death, that suffering and evil are not the final word; life is. In his resurrection we are restored to hope.

> *Response:* Blessed are those who see the light shining in the darkness.

Leader: We unite ourselves with all those who have struggled to find blessings in the midst of losses, with all those who have uncovered saving graces buried in tragedy.

Response: Blessed are those who see the light shining in the darkness.

Naming the Blessings

Music and silent meditation during which the person calls to mind the strengths and blessings that have come from or been developed during an experience of suffering or tragedy, e.g., survival skills during abuse, support experienced during an accident or death.

An empty vase stands on the table with the lighted candle. As the person is ready, he/she names the blessings out loud and places a flower in the vase for each.

Closing Prayer:

Holy Wisdom, we believe that good things sometimes grow and flower in adversity. May we remember and name these blessings as a way of opening to your healing and power. As we continue to struggle against evil, help us not to be conformed to it, but rather to transform what losses we can into riches for our lives. Guide and support us in this mystery, and comfort us with your grace. Amen.

Farewell to an Addiction

You have reached a point of readiness to have done with an addiction. The purpose of this ritual is to demarcate the change in lifestyle and strengthen your resolve.

Opening Prayer: Light a candle and begin:

Gracious God, we open ourselves to your presence here. I call on your assistance as I come to say goodby to an old friend. Thank you for bringing me to this moment. Come to my aid now as I enter into this ritual of separation. I ask this in Jesus' name. Amen.

Reading: Rm 13:11-14, or Col 3:5-11

Play some meditative music as you reflect on the reading and the history of your addiction. Briefly share your thoughts.

Symbolic Rejection of the Addiction

Destroy or at least remove some symbol of the addiction (e.g., bottle, syringe, magazine, photos). Later you can burn or break or bury it, or throw it away.

Gather to yourself symbols of the new means of support you will rely on (e.g., books, photos of friends or support group, meditation, new activities).

> Prayer: O God, I thank you for rescuing me, and for giving me the courage to make this renunciation today. Strengthen my weak knees, and help me to walk without the crutches I have used, which have harmed me far more than they have helped. Forgive me for hurting those I love. Sustain me now with the help of these new resources and friends. I ask it in Jesus' name. Amen.

Consecration

Counselor anoints your forehead with oil, then lays hands on you and prays:

> Great God, in your own image you have made us, crowning us with a divine dignity. Bless this beloved child of yours, and fill him (her) with new life. Awaken in him a keen sense of his infinite value, and sustain him on the path that leads to life. Through Jesus Christ our Lord. Amen.

Close with a song about freedom or new beginning.

Ending a Relationship

You need to end a love relationship, and want to bring closure in a way that blesses and supports you both. You will probably do this ritual by yourselves.

Opening Prayer

Gracious God, we realize we must say goodby, and we ask you to be with us here. Our hearts are filled with many feelings. We thank you for our relationship as well as for our decision to say farewell. Bless our exchange, and help us to say goodby in a way that is good for us both. We ask this through Jesus Christ our Lord. Amen.

Reminiscences

A favorite song

Thank each other, sharing what the relationship has meant. Ask each other's forgiveness, and God's, if appropriate. Recount the reasons for separation.

Reading: 2 Cor 1:3–7, or Jn 14:25–29, or Eccl 3:1–8

Silent reflection

> Prayer: It is time for us, God, to say goodby.
> Thank you for all the moments we have en-
> joyed together, and for all the ways we have
> enriched each other forever. Forgive us for
> any way we have offended you or each
> other. Give us now the strength we need to
> let go of each other and move on. We ask
> this in Jesus' name.

Symbolic Separation

Give back or destroy the symbols and mementos of
the relationship: gifts, photos, letters, etc.

Blessing: Sign each other's foreheads with holy water,
praying:

> God of love, I commend _____ to
> your care. Heal and strengthen him (her).
> Give him the support of faithful friends
> through this difficult period. Grace his path
> with new and wonderful loves. In Jesus'
> name I pray.

Closing Prayer

Thank you, God, for helping us to do this today. Be with each of us now, and help us to keep our resolve. Heal our hearts, and open us to your future. Through Christ our Lord. Amen.

Reconciliation

Opening Prayer

Merciful God, you call us to loving relationship with one another. Be with us now as we seek to heal old wounds and find joy again in this relationship. Replace our hearts of stone with hearts of flesh. Give us the gifts of honesty and openness, and fill us with your healing power and grace. We ask this in Jesus' name.

Reading: Luke 15:11–32

Pause for Silent Prayer

Exchange of Forgiveness

Prayer: Christ Our Friend, open us to the power of your forgiveness. Give us courage to admit that we make mistakes and fail, courage to ask for pardon. Help us to forgive one another freely for all the ways in which we have caused each other pain. Heal the hurt of our words and actions.

Share a simple ritual of forgiveness with one another, using some formula like the following. Each says in turn, "I have hurt you by . . . and I am sorry." The other person replies, "I forgive you as God has forgiven us both."

At the end each gives the other a symbol of new life: a flower, a lighted candle, a card with a picture of a rainbow or flowering tree.

Closing Blessing

May the God of our past, our present and our future be with you today as you make a new beginning.

May God heal the wounds caused by your incomplete attempts at loving, and strengthen your resolve to live in communion.

May God look with mercy on the divisions in our larger world and lead us all to greater understanding.

May your movement toward reconciliation contribute to a universe of peace and love. Amen.

Completion with a Loved One
Who Is No Longer Living

Music and Silent Meditation: Quiet instrumental music while opening to God's presence and calling to mind the loved one. A picture or pictures of that person may be placed in view.

Opening Reading: A candle is lighted. The one saying goodbye brings and shares something that evokes the presence of the person: a poem, meditation, song, inspirational piece, or memorial object.

Letting Go of Regrets and Failures: Time to recall and relinquish what either one might have done or failed to do, perhaps speaking directly to the loved one about these.

> **Prayer:** Risen Christ, enable us to shed the weight of these memories and give up clinging to a past we cannot change. Reach into our lives and give us freedom to embrace our limitations and let go of regrets. You who are our hope from generation to generation, we offer our hearts and the sorrow within them. Mend our brokenness and bless our connections.

Giving Thanks for Positive Memories: Time to recall and share special moments and memories. Gratitude may be expressed directly to the loved one.

> ***Prayer:*** God our Lover and Friend, we give thanks for this person whose love has so enriched our life. Help us to carry his/her blessings as we say goodby and move on. May he/she be an ongoing source of strength and joy.

Planting of Tree or Memorial Garden: The person plants a tree or garden in memory of the loved one. If the ritual takes place indoors, the planting can be done later.

Closing Litany (Based on Revelation 21–22.)

> ***Leader:*** Then I saw a new heaven and a new earth. The first heaven and the first earth had disappeared.

> ***Response:*** I saw the holy city, and the new Jerusalem, coming down from God.

> ***Leader:*** Then I heard a voice from the throne saying, This is the dwell-

ing place of God. Here God dwells among people and wipes away all tears from their eyes.

Response: The One on the throne said: Now I am making the whole of creation new.

Leader: Then I saw the river of life, rising from the throne of God and flowing crystal-clear down the middle of the city.

Response: On either side of the river were trees of life, which bear crops each month of the year and whose leaves are for the the healing of the nations.

Leader: It will never be night again and they will not need lamplight or sunlight, because God will be shining on them.

Response: I am the Alpha and the Omega, the Beginning and the End. Amen.

Sexual Healing

This ritual is for a couple suffering sexual difficulties in marriage as a result of childhood sexual abuse. It comes after individual healing work has taken place, and is done by the couple alone.

Setting: Plan a weekend away in some pleasant place. A few hours before dinner, sit down together in your room, and light a candle.

Opening Prayer:

Gracious God, we ask you to be with us here and to bless us as we enter into this ritual of healing. You have given us the gift of our sexuality, to deepen the bond of our love and create the gift of life. Free us from all that holds us back, so that we can rejoice in the fullness of your goodness to us. We ask this in Jesus' name. Amen.

Sharing: Tell your spouse again in as much detail as you wish about the abuse. Name the ways it has affected you: your feelings about your body, about sexuality, about yourself, about having sex together.

When finished, ask your spouse for any response he (she) may wish to make.

Prayer for Healing

> ***Abuse Survivor:*** I ask you, good God, to heal me in my sexuality. Wash away the effects of the abuse. Free me from whatever keeps me distant from my spouse, whom I love. Let me rejoice in my body, and enjoy and celebrate the gift of my sexuality.

> ***Spouse:*** Thank you, God, for this moment, and for this beautiful person you have given me to be my partner. You have heard her (his) prayer. It is my prayer too. Bring us together sexually, comfortably and joyfully, that our love for each other may be deep and intense. We make these prayers in Jesus' name. Amen.

Reading: Song of Songs 4:1 and 4:9–11, or 8:5–7 Silent reflection

Healing Ritual: Bathe or shower together as a cleansing and renewing action. Then make love.

Closing Prayer:

Gracious God, you have heard our prayer and given us back the gift of our sexual love. We thank you with all our hearts. May we always be at ease with ourselves and with each other, and praise you all our days through the celebration of a passionate love. Through Christ our Lord.

Go out to dinner. Talk about what the experience has meant to you both.

For Ending Counseling

Opening: Light a candle which the person can take home as a reminder of the ritual.

Music and Silent Meditation: Meditative music as a way of entering into the ritual. A time to gather thoughts and feelings about the counseling experience.

Sharing Reflections: What thoughts and feelings came during the silent meditation?

Litany of Thanksgiving: Each shares some of the positive aspects of the counseling as they have experienced or observed them. The other responds. The litany might go something like this:

> **Leader:** For the safety of a place to explore my memories.
>
> **Response:** We give thanks.
>
> **Leader:** For the gift of new insights and understandings.
>
> **Response:** We give thanks.

> **Leader:** For the ability to feel more and hide less of who I am.

> **Response:** We give thanks.

When finished, close with "For these gifts and all that is unspoken, we give thanks."

Exchange of Symbols: If desired, exchange some simple symbol of the relationship, e.g., a rock, a seashell, a card, a copy of the closing blessing.

Closing Blessing of the Person:

> May the giver of gifts and light fill the inmost depths of your heart, and reveal to you the fullness of your beauty and truth.

> May the God who lives in the cells of all life support you in your efforts to walk in ways that are lifegiving for yourself and for all creatures on our planet.

> May the God who has promised to be with us in the valley of darkness, sustain you in moments of doubt, and comfort you in times of pain and sorrow.

May God our healer continue the journey of hope begun in you, allowing you to know seasons of joy and peace, relationships of warmth and faithfulness. Amen.